The Wisdom of Each Other

GROWINGDEEPER

The Wisdom of Each Other

A Conversation Between Spiritual Friends

Eugene H. Peterson

ZondervanPublishingHouse
Grand Rapids, Michigan

A Division of HarperCollins*Publishers*

The Wisdom of Each Other
Copyright © 1998 by Eugene H. Peterson

Requests for information should be addressed to:

📖 ZondervanPublishingHouse
Grand Rapids, Michigan 49530

International Trade Paper Edition ISBN: 0-310-22374-1

Published in association with the literary agency of Alive Communications, Inc., 1465 Kelly Johnson Blvd., Suite 320, Colorado Springs, CO 80920.

Interior design by Sue Koppenol

Printed in the United States of America

98 99 00 01 02 03 04 /❖ DC/ 10 9 8 7 6 5 4 3 2

"I have called you friends . . ."
—JESUS (ST. JOHN 15:15)

CONTENTS

FOREWORD

A favorite story in our home as our children were growing up was of John Muir at the top of the Douglas fir in the storm.* Whenever we were assaulted by thunder and lightning, rain sluicing out of the sky, and the five of us, parents and three children, huddled together on the porch enjoying the dangerous fireworks from our safe ringside seat; one of the kids would say, "Tell us the John Muir story, Daddy!" And I'd tell it again.

In the last half of the nineteenth century, John Muir was our most intrepid and worshipful explorer of the western extremities of our North American continent. For decades he tramped up and down through our God-created wonders, from the California Sierras to the Alaskan glaciers, observing, reporting, praising, and experiencing—entering into whatever he found with childlike delight and mature reverence.

At one period during this time (the year was 1874) Muir visited a friend who had a cabin, snug in a valley of one of the tributaries of the Yuba River in the Sierra Mountains—a place from which to venture into the wilderness and then return for a comforting cup of tea.

One December day a storm moved in from the Pacific—a fierce storm that bent the junipers and pines, the madronas and fir trees as if they were so many blades of grass. It was for just such times this cabin had been built: cozy protection from the harsh elements. We easily imagine

---

*Edwin Way Teale, ed. *The Wilderness World of John Muir* (Boston: Houghton Mifflin, 1954), 181–90.

Muir and his host wrapped in sheepskins, safe and secure in his tightly caulked cabin, a fire blazing against the cruel assault of the elements, Muir meditatively rendering the wildness into his elegant prose. But our imaginations, not trained to cope with Muir, betray us. For Muir, instead of retreating to the coziness of the cabin, pulling the door tight, and throwing another stick of wood on the fire, strode *out* of the cabin into the storm, climbed a high ridge, picked a giant Douglas fir as the best perch for experiencing the kaleidoscope of color and sound, scent and motion, scrambled his way to the top, and rode out the storm, lashed by the wind, holding on for dear life, relishing *Weather:* taking it all in—its rich sensuality, its primal energy.

⌘

Throughout its many retellings, the story of John Muir, storm-whipped at the top of the Douglas fir in the Yuba River valley, gradually took shape as a kind of icon of Christian spirituality for our family. The icon has been in place ever since as a standing rebuke against becoming a mere spectator to life, preferring creature comforts to Creator confrontations.

For spirituality has to do with life, *lived* life. For Christians, "spirituality" is derived (always and exclusively) from Spirit, God's Holy Spirit. And "spirit," in the biblical languages of Hebrew and Greek, is the word "wind," or "breeze," or "breath"—an invisibility that has visible effects.

This is the Wind/Spirit that created all the life we both see and can't see (Genesis 1:2); that created the life of Jesus (Luke 1:35 and 3:22); that created a church of worshiping men and women (Acts 2:2–4); that creates

10

each Christian (Romans 8:11). There is no accounting for life, any life, except by means of this Wind/Spirit:

> *Thou sendest forth thy spirit [breath/wind], they are created:*
> *and thou renewest the face of the earth. (Psalm 104:30 KJV)*

There is clearly far more to Spirit-created living than can be detected by blood pressure and pulse rate. All the "vital signs" of botany, biology, and physiology combined hardly begin to account for life; if it doesn't also extend into matters far more complex than our circulatory and respiratory systems—namely, matters of joy and love, faith and hope, truth and beauty, meaning and value—there is simply not enough there to qualify as "life" for the common run of human beings on this planet earth. Most of us may not be able to define "spirituality" in a satisfactory way, but few of us fail to recognize its presence or absence. And to feel ourselves enhanced by its presence and diminished by its absence. Life, life, and more life—it's our deepest hunger and thirst.

But that doesn't always translate into Spirit, Spirit, and more Spirit in the conduct of our lives. Spirit, *Holy* Spirit, in Christian terminology, is God's life in our lives, God living in us and thereby making us participants in the extravagant prodigality of life, visible and invisible, that is Spirit-created.

We humans, somewhere along the way, seem to have picked up the bad habit of trying to get life on our terms, without all the bother of God, the Spirit of Life. We keep trying to be our own gods; and we keep making a sorry mess of it. Worse, the word has gotten around in recent years that "spirituality" itself might be a way of getting a more intense life without having to deal with God—spirituality as a kind of intuitive bypass around the inconvenience of repentance and sacrifice and putting ourselves at risk by following Jesus in the way of the cross, the very way Jesus plainly told was the only way to the "abundant life" that he had come to bless us with.

The generic name for this way of going about things—trying to put together a life of meaning and security out of God-sanctioned stories and routines, salted with weekends of diversion and occasional erotic interludes, without dealing firsthand, believingly and obediently, with God—is "religion." It is not, of course, a life without God, but the God who is there tends to be mostly background and resource—a Quality or Being that provides the ideas and energy that I take charge of and arrange and use as I see fit. We all of us do it, more or less.

The word "religion," following one possible etymology (not all agree on this), comes from the Latin, *religere*, "to bind up, or tie up, again." The picture that comes to my mind is of myself, having spent years "getting it all together," strolling through John Muir's Yuba River valley, enjoying the country, whistling in self-satisfaction, carrying my "life" bundled in a neat package—memories and morals, goals and diversions, prayers and devotion all sorted and tied together. And then the storm comes, fierce and sudden, a gust tears my packaged life from my arms and scatters the items every which way, all over the valley, all through the forest.

What do I then do? Do I run helter-skelter through the trees, crawl through the brush, frantically trying to recover all the pieces of my life, desperately enlisting the help of passersby and calling in the experts, searching for and retrieving and putting back together again (rebinding!) whatever I can salvage of my life, and then hiding out in the warm and secure cabin until the storm blows over? Or do I follow John Muir to the exposed ridge and the top of the Douglas fir, and open myself to the Weather, not wanting to miss a detail of this invasion of Life into my life, ready at the drop of a hat to lose my life to save it (Mark 8:35)?

For me, the life of religion (cautious and anxious, holding things together as best I can so that my life will make sense and, hopefully, please God) and the life of spirituality (a passion for life and a willingness to risk identity and security in following Jesus, no matter what) contrast in these two scenarios. There is no question regarding what I want: I want to be out in the Weather! But far more often than not I find myself crawling around on the ground, gathering up the pieces of my life and tying them together again in a secure bundle, safe from the effects of the Weather. Actually, the two ways of life can coexist; there is, after all, a place for steady and responsible routine—John Muir, after all, didn't spend all his time at the top of the Douglas fir; he spent most of his time on the valley floor. He also had a cabin that he had built with his own hands in which he received guests and prepared meals for them. But if there is no readiness to respond to the living God, who moves when and how and where he chooses, it isn't much of a life—the *livingness* soon leaks out of it.

⌘

We cannot, of course, command Weather. It is there; it happens. There is no question of managing or directing it. There is no recipe for concocting "spirituality" any more than there is a chemical formula for creating "life."

13

As Jesus most famously put it to that expert on the religious life, Nicodemus, "You know well enough how the wind blows this way and that. You hear it rustling through the trees, but you have no idea where it comes from or where it's headed next. That's the way it is with everyone 'born from above' by the wind of God, the Spirit of God" (John 3:8 THE MESSAGE).

The best we can do is to cultivate awareness, alertness, so that when the Wind blows we are *there*, ready to step into it—or not: when the absurd command comes to distribute the meager five loaves and two fish to the crowd we are ready to obey—or not; when direction is given to wait with the 120 for the promise, we are ready to wait—or not; when the invitation comes to "take . . . eat . . . drink," we are ready to come to the supper—or not.

ᏀᎳᎳᎠ

The books in this series, *Growing Deeper*, are what some of my friends and I do to stay alert and aware as we wait for the Wind to blow whether in furious storm or cooling breeze or gentle breathing—intending to cultivate and maintain a receptive readiness to the Spirit who brings us Life. They are not books *about* spirituality; they are simply accounts of what we do to stay awake to the Coming. There is nothing novel in any of them; our intent is to report what Christians have commonly done to stay present to the Spirit: we pray (Wangerin), preach and teach (Miller), meditate on the soul (Shaw), reflect on our checkered experiences with God's people (Yancey), and nurture Jesus-friends (Peterson).

Our shared conviction is that most of us in this "information age" have adequate access to facts; but in regards to *Life* (*Spirit*-formed spirituality), witness and motivation are always welcome.

Eugene H. Peterson
James Houston Professor of Spiritual Theology
Regent College
Vancouver, B.C., Canada

INTRODUCTION

I was in a conversation recently with a group of friends and mentioned a chance encounter with an odd stranger in which I thought I had heard echoes of the Gospel. It had moved me deeply. One of my friends interrupted, "That sounds good, but I'd like a text for it. Where does the Bible actually say that?" I couldn't come up with a text on the spot. Conversation stopped. A prayerful conversation was trashed because I was not conducting my part in it with the documentation proper to a Bible-study leader.

That happens a lot. And so an entire world of "counsel" between friends is eliminated. Spiritual counsel, easy prayerful conversation between companions engaged in a common task, is less and less frequent. But when Jesus designated his disciples "friends" (John 15:15) in that last extended conversation he had with them, he introduced a term that encouraged the continuing of the conversation. "Friend" sets us in a nonhierarchical, open, informal, spontaneous company of Jesus-friends, who verbally develop relationships of responsibility and intimacy by means of conversation. Characteristically, we do not make pronouncements to one another or look up texts by which to challenge one another; we simply talk out whatever feelings or thoughts are in our hearts as Jesus' friends.

⟨≈≈⟩

Christians set themselves firmly and without apology under the authority of the Word of God—Jesus and the Scriptures that bear witness to him. In our determination to remain faithful to the divine revelation, we sometimes scorn or are dismissive of the less authoritative counsel of companions and friends. Single-mindedness in honoring biblical/gospel authority sometimes means that we don't bother listening to anyone if they are not expounding a text of Scripture.

Ironically, our exclusivity in matters of scriptural authority exposes us to the baleful influences of secularized psychology when we are looking for help in our everydayness. We have no questions about salvation, for there is a text for that. But what do we do when our spouse leaves dirty dishes in the sink or our pastor abandons us for a more attractive post—situations for which there is no text?

I mention this because I get a ton of letters about these very things—spouses and dirty dishes and pastors who disappoint. And I write nearly as many. It is a form of Christian discourse of which I have become very fond. When I step back and reflect on this, it always surprises me, for I am told by experts in the communications industry that letter writing, at least of the kind that I am talking about, is as out of date as the horse-drawn carriage— inefficient, slow, cumbersome. And yet my letter box fills up day after day.

Many of these letters, if not most, have to do in one way or another with the ins and outs of living the Christian life. This also surprises me, for there are any number of men and women who are far more learned than I in these matters and who have written books that are certified classics in the Christian community. If people want to know about these matters, why don't they go to the top? Why don't they go to library or bookstore and get the acknowledged best? They are there for the asking, easily available. And yet my letter box fills up day after day.

But my surprise doesn't ever last long, for I soon realize that there are vast areas in all of our lives in which we care little for either technological efficiency or the latest knowledge. However much we rely on these large boons in getting on in our jobs and keeping up our standard of living, they are not, for the most part, what we live by. We live by small things: gestures, tones, recognitions, attitudes, postcards and letters—friends.

And that is why most of us love getting and writing letters. I don't know many people who do not (getting them, anyway—writing is often another story!). Unlike telephone calls, which often seem like an intrusion, a personal letter invites intimacy.

The first piece of written material that gets read by me is a letter, personally addressed. I may be in the middle of a fascinating novel; I may be energetically involved in working out a piece of scholarship; but when a letter is placed on my desk, personally addressed, I am more likely to read it immediately than not. We want, most of us, to hear what is written to us and to us alone.

❧

The dominant and obvious forms of Christian discourse are preaching and teaching. That is as it should be. We have a great event of salvation to announce to the world—we need to proclaim it clearly and urgently; we have a revealed truth about God and ourselves—we need to make it as plain as possible. But within that large context to which preaching and teaching provide the shape and content there are other ways of using words that are just as important, if not as conspicuous: questions and conversations, comments and ruminations, counsel and suggestion. It is a quieter use of language and mostly takes place in times and places that are not set apart for religious discourse. It often conveys as much in what is not said as in what is. Marked by hesitancies and asides, it rarely strikes a pose of authoritative boldness, which we rightly expect from our preachers and teachers.

The usual phrase to designate these informal, unplanned exchanges in the Christian community is "spiritual counsel." Spiritual counsel doesn't speak with the authority of preaching; and it isn't capable of the precision of teaching. In the verbal triad of biblical speech, it necessarily occupies a far more modest place—reticent, shy, awkward. In fact, I am reluctant to use the phrase "spiritual counsel," for the phrase might carry connotations of "elevated" or "holy." And far more often than not it consists of apparently nonurgent, nonreligious concerns. Just the day-by-day business of following Jesus, one step after another, wondering how on earth the Holy Spirit is bringing anything worthy of being called fruit out of the gravel and weeds of *my* life, and listening, when we think of it, for the whispering of the Spirit in local mulberry trees and people. If disaster strikes—accident or illness or loss—a faithful pastor or godly friend can usually be trusted to show up with a well-thumbed Bible and set what we are experiencing squarely within the large structures of Providence.

But how about those long stretches of "ordinary time"? The conversations that take place in the parking lot after Sunday worship are as much a part of the formation of Christian character as the preaching from the sanctuary pulpit. The small talk that accumulates around the ritual of putting children to sleep for the night is as sacred as the most solemn of eucharistic liturgies. Most of our lives, after all, are *not* in crisis. We also need ways of conversing about our lives in Christ.

But conversation, as such, though honored by our ancestors, is much neglected today as a form of Christian discourse. If we are to be in touch with all the parts of our lives and all the dimensions of the Gospel, conversation requires equal billing (although not equal authority) with preaching and teaching.

When conversation takes written form, it is usually by letter—a personal letter addressed "Dear Anne," signed with your name and sent to a place on the map with a named or numbered street. Most of such letters are modestly conceived, but not infrequently their effects far exceed our intentions. The first documents that entered our New Testament (St. Paul's letters), came into existence in exactly this way.

Gunnar Thorkildsson, the recipient of the following letters, is not an actual person with an existence documented by birth certificate and social security number. But he is nevertheless quite real. I haven't "made up" anything about him. All the details of his life, his *soul*, and my responses to them come from actual encounters with men and women who do have birth certificates and social security numbers. For convenience (and confidentiality) I have addressed my letters to Gunnar. Virtually the only difference between these letters and the others that I write is that I didn't have to buy postage stamps to send them.

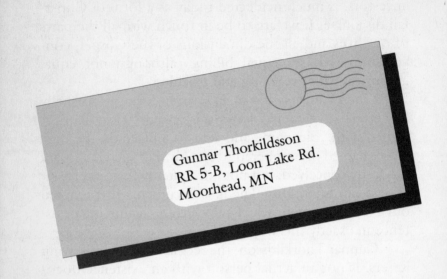

Gunnar Thorkildsson
RR 5-B, Loon Lake Rd.
Moorhead, MN

*D*ear Gunnar,

I must say that your letter caught me by complete surprise, but also with considerable delight. After all these years! From time to time someone or other would mention your name, but I never got enough accompanying gossip to give me any sense of your life, so the forty years since we last saw each other at university graduation are a virtual silence.

It is true, as you say, that we have lived very different lives. But I wonder how different, really. Externally different, to be sure: you wandering the face of the earth with your large doubts, I working the small acreage of my parish, husbanding my small faith; you leaving the Faith, I staying in it. But as I read your letter, I could still hear the cadence of your voice in those sentences and could feel again the old intimacies of spirit that we experienced in the years of our growing up together and that made us such fast friends.

So maybe our lives have not been so different after all. For both of us, God has held the center of our awareness and action. The contrast between your shaking your fist at him and my shaking hands with him may not be as significant as that it is God who has dominated both of our lives; we have both known that it is God with whom we have been dealing from start to finish. Your statement "There has hardly been a moment when I haven't been aware of the God against whom I protested so much" struck me as ironic: you in your unbelieving have probably thought about God more than I have in my believing. Companions relax and take many things for granted; competitors have to be constantly on the alert.

I like the way you put it: "I've finally decided to quit competing with God and join him." Do you realize how biblically you have phrased your decision? For life's basic decision is rarely, if ever, whether to believe in God or not, but whether to worship or compete with him. The biblical word in this context for competition is usually "idolatry."

At any rate, it is going to be interesting to resume our old conversations after this forty-year silence between us, a silence in which we each have been preoccupied, in our differing ways and circumstances, with God.

The peace of the Lord,
Eugene

————————————————————

*D*ear Gunnar,

You are fortunate to have found a congregation of Christians to join up with. And so soon. Especially since you had such an accumulation of negative experiences of church early on. Wasn't that the primary factor in sending you off into your years of wilderness wandering? But you're quite right: you could be a solitary wanderer; you can't be a solitary Christian.

It amuses me to imagine the two of us, so different and yet so alike, you putting down new roots mid-continent, with me perched a little precariously on its western extremity, the taut forty-ninth parallel both separating and connecting us. I anticipate that we will find far more connection than separation.

The peace of the Lord,
Eugene

_____

*D*ear Gunnar,

Well, that didn't last long, did it? I mean your romance with the church. Did you so easily forget that it is *sinners* that God calls to repentance, and that a lot of them, having heard the call and decided that they like the sound of the good news of salvation, somewhere along the way ditch the repentance part? And now you find yourself involved in a company of friends to whom you are not feeling very friendly.

You say that you have almost nothing in common with these people. But isn't that just the point? *You* have nothing in common with them; but *God* does. This just happens to be the way that God goes about making a kingdom, pulling all sorts and conditions of people together and then patiently, mercifully, and graciously making something of them. What he obviously does not do is pre-select people who have an aptitude for getting along well and enjoying the same things. Of course you don't have much in common with them. The church is God's thing, not yours.

You told me earlier that your motive for returning to the Christian way was that you had tried being your own god all these years, "gave it your best shot" you said, and made a thorough mess of it. And wasn't one of your primary strategies in that enterprise deliberately associating only with people with whom you had something in common? You said it was a matter of integrity. And look what happened—you left your first wife because you no longer had anything in common with her; your second wife left you because she no longer had anything in common with you. And how many jobs have you abandoned because you had "grown out of them"? Because of your extraor-

26

dinary competence as a scientist you never had any trouble getting another, and usually better, post. But your insistence on emotional or intellectual or vocational camaraderie on your terms has left you today with neither family nor friends.

And now you are back at it, second-guessing God's way of being God. You have had a lot of arguments with God through the years and tell me that you have lost most of them. Why not give up on this one too and just let God do it his way? The church is not a natural community composed of people with common interests; it is a *super*-natural community. And the *super* in that word does not mean that it exceeds your expectations; it is *other* than your expectations, and much of the other is invisible to you as yet.

I'm sorry if I am sounding a bit sharp-tongued on this, but I don't want you getting off on the wrong foot in this church business. Trust me, there's a lot more going on than you will ever have in common with anyone there. Go back to the company of those seventy or eighty people on Sunday, listen believingly to the Scriptures read and preached, offer your prayers, receive Jesus in the sacrament, and bless your neighbors. And wait for the Kingdom. It's the Holy Spirit's style to fashion holy lives among the inept.

The peace of the Lord,
Eugene

———————————

*D*ear Gunnar,

No, you don't have to like the hymns. And yes, you do need to sing them—hopefully in approximate tune and rhythm with the rest. It's an excellent exercise in humility.

The peace of the Lord,
Eugene

———————————

*D*ear Gunnar,

Your memory is quite accurate; I *was* very suspicious of the word "spiritual" in my younger years. I'm still suspicious. I think my suspicions were first aroused by hanging around that religious conference place, Shiloh Center, half way down the lake, that you and I used to look in on from time to time. We were attracted to the place, as I remember, by the intensity of the people and the electricity in the air. Such a spiritual place! Such spiritual people! If you didn't use the word "spiritual" in the first thirty seconds of your conversation you were a marked person—Not-Very-Spiritual. Phrases like "deeper life" and "second blessing" gave off intimations of ecstasy, and as excitable adolescents we were susceptible to anything that smacked of adventure, especially when it also hinted at initiating us into an upper class of Christians at the same time.

You were quicker than I was at noticing the lack of continuity between the ecstasies at the Center and everyday life back in town. But I too caught on after awhile. The mothers of our friends who were bitchy before were bitchy still. Mr. Billington, our history teacher, held in such veneration at the Center for his visions and prophecies, never relinquished his position in the high school as the most mean-spirited of all our teachers.

I started applying the 1 John 4:8 test ("Whoever does not love does not know God . . .") to spiritual people, and it was surprising how many of them rated at best a C-minus. But grading the condition of people's souls is a risky business. It doesn't take much imagination to realize how quickly you could lose your own soul in the process. So I quit grading.

But I've retained a wariness of "spiritual" and use the word as little as possible. Too often it seems to signal a split between sacred and secular, between inside and out-side, between a refined religious sensibility and the coarser necessities of ordinary life like changing diapers, paying bills, and giving good weight in a job you feel stuck with. For as long as "spiritual" carries these elitist connotations in popular speech, I will use the word as sparingly as possible.

Now that you have re-entered the Christian community after such a long absence, you may find that you are also having to re-examine the Christian vocabulary for accuracy and honesty. We Christians can't be too careful about the words we use and the way we use them.

The peace of the Lord,
Eugene

———————————————

*D*ear Gunnar,

Well, the British Columbia winter rains have begun—and now the prospect of several months of Canadian drizzle and mist and fog. Actually, I have come to like these long stretches of rainy weather. There is a kind of austerity and earthiness that accompanies it that always seems to me to throw a wet blanket on the illusion-fueled and ego-swollen expectations of our culture, whether secular or religious. We have so little encouragement to cultivate emptiness, that when the weather does it for us, it strikes me as a gift. Without self-emptying, how can we be ready for Spirit-filling?

The peace of the Lord,
Eugene

Dear Gunnar,

When you ask me how to begin a spiritual life, I think I know what you mean. You want, I take it, to live the Christian life intentionally and not haphazardly, firsthand and not conventionally. But the phrasing is askew: *you* don't begin the spiritual life, the Holy Spirit does. And it began a long time ago. It was His idea before it was yours.

So the question is not primarily "What do I do?" but rather "What has the Holy Spirit been doing in me all these years of my noncooperation and what is He doing still?" I hope I can be of help in recognizing and naming this work of God the Spirit in you. But my primary help is going to be in preventing you from taking on the Christian life as your project. God has already taken you on— you are His project.

This may seem like a quibble, but it is not. Most of us fall into the trap from time to time. We become Christians because we realize we cannot save ourselves and need Christ to save us. But once we are "in" we start taking over the job.

What is essential is to know that the Christian life is mostly what is being done to you, not what you are doing. William Meredith's poem "Chinese Banyan" gets it right:

> *I speak of the unremarked*
> *Forces that split the heart*
> *   And make the pavement toss—*
> *Forces concealed in quiet*
> *   People and plants . . .*

We all of us need frequent reminding of this. This is my first reminder, but it won't be my last.

The peace of the Lord,
Eugene

---

*D*ear Gunnar,

I'm glad that you had such a good time at the international conference for prayer and the spiritual life. I'm sure it was exhilarating for you to be with Christians from all over the world, sharing their enthusiasm, their deep hunger and thirst after God. Moments like that are precious. I'm glad that you were able to go.

There is something analogous to the Day of Pentecost in such gatherings—hearing all these voices from so many different cultures and languages praising God. The sense that the whole world is giving voice to our Savior's praise.

But I am a little alarmed that you are planning to go to another similar gathering in six months. Conferences on the spiritual life are wonderful—occasionally. I think *very* occasionally. They do not provide the substance for a life of obedient faith. They contribute almost nothing, maybe even less than nothing, to a life of spiritual maturity. They are stimulus. Appetizer. They are not nutritious. High in fat, low in protein.

If they become a staple in your spiritual formation, they only distract and dilute. When you next feel the need for some outside encouragement and refreshment, you would do better to book a three day vacation in Hawaii. Lie on the beach and soak in creation.

The reason is that the Christian life is thoroughly organic—the Holy Spirit grows the spiritual life in you, forms Christ's life in you, in the particular conditions in which *you* live—Minnesota weather, rural culture, estranged wives, stand-offish children, comfortable income, and a still uncomfortable Lutheran liturgy.

If you go to Singapore and are blessed, that is great. But don't suppose that the experience is reproducible in Moorhead. Authentic spirituality is not transferable. It is not a franchise—some of those people seem to think you can set up its golden arches any old place they target a market for it.

The peace of the Lord,
Eugene

---

*D*ear Gunnar,

Yes, I think it is both proper and essential to pray for what you designate Big Things. We don't want prayer, the largest and most inclusive action of which we are capable, to be confined to getting us safely across the street and staying out of moral mud puddles. Jesus got us started well when he posted God's Name and Kingdom and Will at the top of our prayer list.

So praying to our Sovereign God for City and Country, President and Mayor obviously does not exceed our mandate. What I think we need to remember, though, is that when we pray for the Big Things, God's responses commonly come in small and hidden ways, at least in ways we think of as small and hidden. Praying for the City, a Big Thing, may have no visible effects on the City as reported in the newspapers and on TV. God looks at things very differently than we do. Our task is to pray ardently and faithfully; we cannot assume that we know how the prayer will be answered.

I've always loved the phrase in George Bernanos' *Diary of a Country Priest*: "Just think! The Word was made Flesh—and not a journalist in the world wrote it up!" (By the way, if you haven't yet read this book, get it; there is much wisdom in it.)

The peace of the Lord,
Eugene

---

*D*ear Gunnar,

I know exactly what you felt at that study group. Last night I had a similar experience. I had been invited to give a guest lecture at the university; later I sat in on one of the discussion groups that followed. The discussion was dominated by two men in their early twenties who didn't see me sitting off in the shadows. They spent the hour ignorantly, brashly, and bullyingly interrupting the others and criticizing anything that hinted of prayer or Catholicism or mysticism. Bulldozer spirituality. I get mighty tired of it.

The peace of the Lord,
Eugene

———————————

*D*ear Gunnar,

I am in complete sympathy with the difficulty you are having in establishing a habit of prayer. Among Christians, disciplined prayer tops the charts in the listings of failed resolutions—resolutions congealing into procrastination and guilt.

The one thing I don't want to do as I respond to you is add to the guilt. Believe me, I have put in my time too in the ranks of try-and-fail, start-and-quit, resolve-and-procrastinate.

We live in jerky times, assaulted by "urgent" demands. For most of our ancestors in the Christian way, Scripture and prayer were embedded in routine and validated by social structures. Today those routines have been replaced by fax and telephone.

Two hundred years ago it was not at all uncommon for Christian barbers, carpenters, homemakers, and farmers to spend an hour or two every day at their prayers. Today, I am happy if I can get my contemporaries to spend five minutes at them while commuting to work or waiting for the wash cycle to be completed at the Laundromat or sitting with a cup of coffee at break time. The old wisdom in this is "pray as you can, not as you can't." In matters like this, at least in the beginning stages, it is not quantity that counts mostly. It was our Lord, after all, who gave us images of seeds and salt to work with—it doesn't take much of either to make a huge difference.

For someone like you, lacking a lifetime of habit and routine in Scripture and prayer, the best strategy is to start small. What I am saying, I guess, is that you shouldn't take on the burden of single-handedly going against the whole culture. Infiltrate brief prayers into the interruptions and noise. I had a friend years ago who always bought inexpensive Bibles; each morning he ripped out a fresh page, stuck it in his shirt pocket, and at odd times through the day pulled it out and read a few lines at a time. When he finished he crumpled it up and threw it in the trash. It sounded like sacrilege when he first told me; on reflection it seemed more like good espionage work.

The peace of our Lord,
Eugene

———————————————

Dear Gunnar,

Well, yes—there is a lot more to it than that. Prayer is at the very center of our being as believers in and followers of Jesus. Our intent is that it encompass and penetrate everything that we do and are. St. Paul's "pray without ceasing" is what we're after. That is obvious, I think.

What is not obvious is that you can't make it happen by sheer will power or by working up time-management charts in which you schedule in prayer in increasing amounts.

What I would like to do right now is to get you out of the driver's seat. Prayer is the work of the Holy Spirit in you. You certainly play a part in it, but not the main part.

The single most important thing to know about prayer is that Jesus prays, *is praying right now*, and for you. The large, revealed fact that Jesus prays is the reality in which you and I learn to do our praying. My life of prayer is not primarily a matter of what I do or don't do, but of what Jesus does—*is doing*, "at the right hand of God the Father."

Here's my suggestion: Read and ponder John 17 and Hebrews 7:24–25 for the next two or three weeks. Jesus is praying. Live meditatively in this reality: "Jesus is praying—for me." Relax. Don't be so anxious about getting better at prayer. Jesus is on the job and he's not going to get tired or bored and quit on you.

After you have had some time to accommodate your imagination to this huge fact, we can begin talking about your part in it. But take your time—this is going to take awhile.

The peace of the Lord,
Eugene

———————————

*D*ear Gunnar,

I took a walk this morning down to the beach. I do this two or three times a week. In the early morning I usually have the place to myself. I sit on a peace of driftwood and take in the world of mountain and water, sky and weather. And the birds. I watch and admire the birds: goldeneyes, buffleheads, usually a great blue heron, mallards, gulls, ravens, and an occasional bald eagle. The intricate intersections of beauty make a fine warp for my prayers.

This morning there was something added: a bulldozer cleaning logs off the beach, logs that had drifted in, storm tossed, through the winter months. It was outfitted with an ingenious device at the front end that could pick up the logs and deposit them neatly in a pile. It was noisy and jerky. The acrid diesel exhaust stank up the beach.

And here's what struck me: The noisy, stinking bulldozer had attracted eight or ten men and women spectators, standing around talking, obviously fascinated with this exercise of technological prowess. But why hadn't I seen any of these people before? The montage of weather and birds, driftwood and sand, sky and water was far more beautiful and far more full of mystery than this contraption of steel belching poison gas. Why would anyone routinely boycott the daily winter light show and bird ballet on the beach, and then show up at an inconvenient hour to attend to this hulk of noise and stink?

I guess I know the answer, and so do you. But I realize how vigilant we have to be to keep a fascination with technology from intruding and taking over our prayers and our love.

Is this the way you felt attending that prayer work-shop in Chicago? I thought it might be.

The peace of the Lord,
Eugene

---

*D*ear Gunnar,

You do insist on using this word "spiritual" don't you. Overusing, I'd say. We have very different feelings about this word—you obviously like it a lot more than I do.

I wonder if it isn't because of the quite different worlds that we have been living in? You in a very secularized world—laboratories and instruments, computers and scientific reports. And I in the world of religion—prayer and worship, funerals and baptisms.

Your world has been pretty totally defined by the rational and technological. And while that held great attraction for you for a long time, you ended up feeling stifled—reduced to explanations and techniques. You wrote me once that you felt that all the life had been squeezed out of you by the know-it-alls and the do-it-alls. You longed for breathing room. And so every time you heard the word "spiritual," regardless of context, you caught an intimation of life and breath, a witness to the reality of the innerness that you missed so much.

And then you returned to the Christian way and found those witnesses confirmed in the Holy Spirit— more "innerness" than you had ever thought possible. So of course you like the word "spiritual." For you the word served as a distant flare on the horizon during your long trek through the murk and gloom of reductionist rationalism and technology. And now that the "Dayspring from on high" has appeared for you, you remember the flares with fondness. I can understand that.

For me, the word has very different associations. My world has been defined by the Trinity: God the Father revealed in Jesus the Son by the Holy Spirit. Spirit is God's Spirit, bringing God's life. Unlike you, who felt constricted and reduced, I have felt invited into largeness and openness. Whereas you associated primarily with people who took on life as a problem to be solved, I have cultivated company with those who enter it as a mystery to be explored.

But in this company, unfortunately, there are also numerous men and women who want the vitality and ecstasy of spirit without dealing with the Holy Spirit who reveals God in Jesus. These are the ones who are forever talking about being "spiritual" and how to be "more spiritual." Spirituality then becomes an elitist activity, a kind of snobbish Christian sub-culture with its own gurus and lore. And do you know what they end up doing? Hauling in truckloads of rationalism and technology from the world you have so recently abandoned in order to be more spiritual! No more mystery. And only as much of God as they think they need to legitimize their spiritual selfism. Can you understand why I get a little tired of the word "spiritual"?

I think I may be on to something here—why you like the word and why I avoid it. What do you think?

The peace of the Lord,
Eugene

———————————

*D*ear Gunnar,

I wish you would quit regretting your long defection from the Faith. Regret is the most useless of all the religious emotions and nearly the opposite of repentance, with which it is often confused.

What I think would be much more appropriate for you would be to *relish* your status as a layperson and see all those years of immersion in the "world" as your graduate education in it, much as Melville used to designate his years on the whaling ships as his "Harvard and Yale." Instead of regretting that you didn't spend those years being trained in theology and exegesis, appreciate the education you *did* get—a thorough training in laity-ness.

For even though you weren't giving God much of your life those years, at least in a believing way, he was spending considerable time and effort on you the whole time. Now that you have your degree, let's see how he will use you.

The peace of the Lord,
Eugene

———————————————

*D*ear Gunnar,

I don't think you can ever be too detailed in your prayers, too specific, too minute. I don't think Jesus' remarks about having the hairs of your head numbered and keeping track of every sparrow that falls were hyperbolic in the least. Understatements, if anything. We're involved, remember, in a way of life in which God in Jesus has immersed himself in the details of our living. We are not dealing on the front line with grand general truths and cosmic metaphysics, but with daily bread and ingrown toenails and forgiving the rude behavior of an old friend.

I've always liked the remark I picked up out of a newspaper interview with the Chicago architect, Frank Sullivan: "God is in the details." Or maybe it was "divinity is in the details." Anybody, he was saying, can draw up grand schemes, towering monuments, stunning skyscrapers, ornate mansions. But it takes someone who knows what he or she is doing to designate the proper place for each bolt, determine the exact stress required of a girder, design the building to fit the actual weather and landscape of the terrain.

You can't develop your understanding and practice of prayer in reaction to that dreadful woman with whom you seem to be stuck in making your weekly hospital visits—that one who always prays for a parking place (and gets it!) but who treats the hospital orderlies with such undisguised contempt. Her mistake is not in praying too much but in insufficient detail. Actually, in praying for the parking place, she is probably praying for the biggest thing in her life at the moment; the orderlies, consigned as she supposes to the curbs of "outer darkness," have no power to either add or subtract from her creature comforts and therefore are too "small" to get included in her prayers. Her problem is not small prayers but a small life.

By the way, you haven't remarked on how these weekly hospital visits with the deacons to the sick and dying are going. You wrote that you felt after spending so much of your life cultivating the company of the powerful, you felt the need to get in touch with the world of the weak. Is that working out the way you thought it might?

The peace of our Lord,
Eugene

—————————————

*D*ear Gunnar,

I can appreciate the devastation you feel on discovering the false life of that pastor over in North Dakota that you admired so much. But I wonder if it is quite the disaster you suppose it to be? I think it might even be a good thing (not the disaster, but you having to deal with it). You are still pretty new at the daily working conditions of this Christian life and have a tendency to look up to those who have "reputations." Our whole age encourages it—giving the status of expert to anyone with a fairly good track record and the glow of celebrity.

But it is never a good idea, and the sooner we are cured the better. I remember once as a seminarian that I had become completely captivated by a theologian who seemed to me to embody everything that a theologian should be. He knew everything, had thought through everything, was conversant with all the ins and outs of the "present evil age," and was able to re-say the Christian faith in ways that were both profoundly true and immediately understandable—and in a German accent no less! And then I found out that he was a compulsive philanderer and a dabbler in pornography. I stormed into the study of my pastor, striking a tragic pose, and said, "I'm totally disillusioned!" He slapped his hand on his desk and said, "Good! Who wants to go around stuck with a bunch of illusions! Jesus is not going to disillusion you."

Initially, I was put off by his lack of sympathy but since then have appreciated his wisdom. He was right. We are in a fight for truth and God-reality—illusions are dangerous in this business. We need to know the human heart and the surrounding culture as they are, deceitfully wicked and infested with prowling lions.

The Christian life is not romantic. And it certainly doesn't assume the best in everyone—particularly preachers. In some ways we assume the worst, but without despair, for it is because of this "worst" that we are in the salvation business, not out selling religious cosmetics.

The peace of our Lord,
Eugene

_____

*D*ear Gunnar,

I think you are ready for a theologian. I mean a *real* theologian. Especially in this secularizing culture we live in, when virtually all our mental habits are formed by people training us to get what we think we have coming to us and looking out for the big chance, we desperately need men and women at our side who have disciplined their minds to think *God*: who God is and what he is doing in and among us; what it means to be created and chosen by God and how we get in on what he intends for us. We need help, most of us, in thinking, not just *about* God, but in terms of God, with God as our presupposition.

When we start taking the Christian life seriously, as you have, it necessarily, of course, involves taking *ourselves* seriously. But most of us then get distracted from our main task by taking ourselves more seriously than God. And God is our primary concern, not us.

I know that theology is not stylish in this generation of Christians. When our friends think of going for help for their souls, they usually think in terms of their feelings and egos—their innerness, their hearts—and quite naturally gravitate to counselors, psychologists, and psychiatrists—something along the lines of the therapeutic.

But in matters of the Christian life, and especially prayer, it is the theologian we want at our side, to help us *start* with God, not just end up with God as a court of last resort.

If you're trying to understand yourself, go ahead and consult a psychologist, but if it's God you're after, get a theologian. Many of the difficulties in prayer come from paying too much attention to ourselves—our moods, our feelings, our fitness to pray. But prayer is paying attention to God. We Christians need theologians far more than we need psychologists. Keep a therapist/counselor in the wings for those times when you need help untangling your self from yourself, but make sure you get a theologian to walk by your side.

The peace of our Lord,
Eugene

———————————————————

*D*ear Gunnar,

Your visit to that bookstore was quite a disaster, wasn't it? You came home so excited, with all those books. What was it you spent? A hundred and twenty seven dollars? You thought you had hit the mother lode! All this *Christian* stuff being written more or less behind your back while all these years you had been off reading your technical journals and diverting yourself with an occasional murder mystery. And then the disappointment of finding that you had purchased nothing but extended cheerleader slogans written in bad prose.

I'm sorry to have to tell you that during the forty years that you were off doing your own thing, having concluded that religion was for ninnies, a considerable number of people in North America wondered whether religion could be marketed as a consumer product for just such ninnies. Some of them started writing books from that angle, and, sure enough, they were right. Writing in the market-tested style that so effectively sells automobiles and deodorants, they were similarly successful. Their basic strategy is to locate an area of dissatisfaction in modern life, and then promise God, or something that has to do with God, as the solution.

The unhappy results of a half-century of this sort of thing are piled up, unread, on your desk right now. I'm sorry; I should have warned you.

The good news is that the good books are still around. It sometimes takes a little effort to find them, but they are there. But you're not likely to find them displayed prominently in the bookstores, particularly under the sections titled, "Inspirational," or "Devotional." When browsing in a bookstore and finding one of my books displayed in these sections, I sometimes surreptitiously remove it from the shelf and insert it among, "Cookbooks"—I think I'm more likely to find a spiritual readiness for the uniqueness of the Christian message among those who are dealing with the basics of daily existence than among those who are trying to escape them.

Why don't you sit down with your pastor and work up a list of a dozen or so books that you can read and re-read over the next couple of years? Your remedial education in Christian belief and practice.

The peace of the Lord,
Eugene

*D*ear Gunnar,

You realize, don't you, that nothing in the Christian life can be imposed from without. I know you are impatient to make up for lost time, but there are no shortcuts in this business. The life of Christ emerges from within the actual circumstances of our seemingly very unspiritual lives—the daily stuff of ordinariness and accidents and confusion, good days and bad days, taking the humdrum and the catastrophic both in stride.

There are miracles aplenty in this life, but most Christian miracles (not all) don't take the form of interventions but are hidden in circumstances of fear and betrayal and disillusion, kids who don't behave and friends who disappoint. Mangers and crosses. And all the time a *life*, a Christ-life, is being formed that is fully human.

I am, I guess, asking you to join me in a protest against all "pious" spirituality—what I think of as boutique spirituality—and deal in Jesus' name with the daily stuff that comes our way with robust prayer and dogged obedience.

The peace of our Lord,
Eugene

―――――――――――――――

*D*ear Gunnar,

You are quite right in not looking to me for answers, since I have a pretty low credit rating in that department. But it's just fine to want and expect companionship in the Way. And conversation. Holy conversation.

We're several weeks ahead of you in getting Spring, but yours is coming too. It always does, both inside and outside. The violet-green swallows are at this moment swooping in and out of my vision from here in my study, arcing through the air, filling it with motions of beauty. There is a succession of wildflowers—about every two weeks one set fades and withers and another is there to take its place. Hiking in the mountains over the weekend we found prairie smoke and stonecrop and silky lupine on parade. And we saw our first harebell in the woods yesterday.

The peace of our Lord,
Eugene

———————————————

*D*ear Gunnar,

So, your friends are trying to turn you into a religious consumer, are they, inviting you to their wonderful churches where so much exciting stuff is going on? I would resist it. You're better off sticking with what you started out with at your Christian re-entry—the "smallest and nearest church." It's still my standard counsel in churchgoing. Of course, I admit exceptions, but not for the reasons your friends are setting out. Those several dozen phlegmatic Norwegians, dozing under the liturgical inexpertness of your young pastor, are as good company as any with whom to listen to God's word and worship his holy name.

Where did all this frenzy in "looking for a good church" get started, anyway? Certainly not from any passion for holy obedience among the "least of these my brethren." This church-shopping mentality, where we expect to find a flavor to suit every taste, is spiritually destructive. I don't see any good coming out of church worship that caters to our *taste* in worship.

The peace of our Lord,
Eugene

––––––––––––––––––––

Dear Gunnar,

The general rule in these matters is cautious but quiet skepticism. We certainly do not want to be party to rejecting anything that the Holy spirit is doing. The "Gamaliel Rule" (Acts 5:34–39) is in place to prevent that. But our experienced ancestors noticed that the paranormal in spiritual things is far more often the work of the Devil than the Spirit.

If the devil can distract us from the "one thing needful" by getting us absorbed in mere phenomena, that is as effective as seducing us into an adulterous affair and has the added benefit of tricking us into thinking that we are superspiritual. From the Devil's point of view, tempting someone like you to gross sins is a risky business, for chances are the consequent guilt would send you to your repentant knees, seeking forgiveness. But by introducing spiritual sins into our lives, he more often than not, besides distracting us, is able to introduce dissension and confusion into the community and puff us up, if ever so slightly, with an insider's pride.

You are not, you know, required to have an opinion or take a stand in these matters—we are not dealing with either faith or morals. Why don't you, instead, make a list of three or four people whom you know to be lonely, and while your friends are going to these meetings, go visit these souls regularly for the next three months, listening to them and praying with them. My idea is that you deliberately substitute an extraordinary act of love in Jesus' name for what may be only feverish spiritual voyeurism.

The peace of our Lord,
Eugene

*D*ear Gunnar,

I realized this morning how pleased I am that you invited me into your life, participating in the praying, listening, talking, writing as the Spirit does the work of love and forgiveness and obedience—even though two thousand miles and four decades of silence separate us. Even with all the sense of homecoming and grace that you have, I know, too, that there are many slow days when nothing seems to be happening. A lot of the Christian life develops "underground" when we aren't looking.

The rhythm of life has slowed here. We bought a new canoe in May. I made one twenty-five years ago, but it is battered and bruised pretty badly, so we decided it was time to give it a decent burial and get a new one. This one is so much smoother. We go out in the quiet and muted colors of evening and feel the fragility of our lives and the canoe held in the immensity of sky and mountains and water. A canoe is a perfect vehicle for contemplation. Often you unobtrusively enter my prayers at those times and I sense ripples of hope and blessing.

The peace of our Lord,
Eugene

---

*D*ear Gunnar,

I'm not at all pleased with the list of books you and your pastor came up with. I meant for you to start reading *theology*, not books on spiritual trend-setting and religious motivation. I meant the Masters. It appears to me that your pastor has a very low opinion of your mental capabilities and little respect for your vocation. It is a very condescending list.

I think I know what happened. Your pastor, as much as I like him from what you have told me of him and as well-intentioned as he undoubtedly is, looks at you through the filter of *layperson* and sees a person who has to be initiated into thinking about God. As if God were some advanced form of knowledge, like calculus, that you have to be schooled in with prerequisites before you can be trusted with the subject.

Let's not blame your pastor—most of his professional pastor and priest colleagues on this continent do the same thing. *Layperson,* for them, is a term designating not an honored vocational condition or setting but a spiritual inadequacy, which it is their job to make less inadequate through their promotional and educational efforts. Unthinkingly, some pastors think that they can make you a better Christian by making you more like themselves.

I say, unthinkingly, because a fairly cursory observation is enough to bring up plenty of evidence that the pastor is no better at the *Christian* business, as such, than the parishioners. We're all in this together, needing each other, praying for each other, forgiving and serving one another. "Pastor" is not an advanced form of "Christian"—you don't have to hang around churches and pastors very long to find that out.

But don't read anything anticlerical into my words. "Pastor" is honorable work, and very important to the Christian community. I am one, myself, remember—and have been one for about as long as you have been a scientist. But your pastor's work is not to train you to think and work like a pastor so that you can preach a sermon, conduct a liturgy, and negotiate your way through congregational management and church finances any more than yours is to train him to think and work like a scientist so that he can get along adequately in a world of entropy and neutrons and quasars.

We each have our proper work by which in Jesus' name we *serve* one another, not recruit one another to run errands for us. St. Paul was quite eloquent on the subject, which shows that the confusion has been around a long time. Those books may very well be important to his work, but I can't see that they have anything to do with yours. And not one of them qualifies as theology.

The peace of the Lord,
Eugene

———————————————

*D*ear Gunnar,

Sorry, in my irritation at the widespread clerical condescension to the laity, I digressed and forgot to direct you to a proper theologian.

Why not start at the top? Start with John Calvin. Among Christians of our ilk, he continues to hold the center for biblical soundness and intellectual clarity. Buy *The Institutes of the Christian Religion*. It comes in two volumes. Make sure you get the translation by John McNeill.

If you're troubled by dust balls of opinion on Calvin that you have picked up through hearsay through the years, do your best to sweep them out with the trash—come to him fresh with a clean imagination. You'll be surprised at how accessible he is, how sane, how *Christian*. A truly elegant intellect.

Of course, as with anyone writing several centuries ago in another language and culture (sixteenth century, French and Latin) there are many allusions that you will miss and not a few pages that you will pass over rather quickly. But mostly, you can expect to be directed wisely and prayerfully to God—thinking about God accurately, responding to God truly. Calvin brought a biblically disciplined mind and a Spirit-attuned heart to his writing.

And he was a pastor, first and foremost a pastor with a congregation whom he taught and prayed for, visited, baptized and married and buried, whose problems he dealt with and whose faith he guided. He was writing for Christians like you who are trying to get a clear sense of God's revelation in the cultural/religious murk of a very messed-up society—messed up mentally and morally. He was *not* writing a text for use in graduate schools and seminaries. He was *not* writing a source book for doctoral dissertations. He was writing so that every-day Christians with jobs and families could think and say the words "God" and "Jesus" and "Spirit" cleansed from all the misleading distortions and superstitions that we pick up in church street-talk.

I guess what I want to convince you of up front is that real theologians don't make God more complicated but less. They clear the ground. They simplify our lives, not clutter them. So don't be intimidated by the big names. If you can read the editorial page of the Wall Street Journal with understanding, you can read Calvin. That writer that you like so much, Flannery O'Connor, after washing her face and brushing her teeth each night, used to read a couple of pages of Thomas Aquinas before going to sleep, to, as she put it, "give my mind a good scrubbing."

But this warning: you don't come to God by thinking but by praying. Thinking rightly about God in itself doesn't get us where we want to go. But bad thinking can mess us up considerably. The task of the theologian is not primarily to teach us to think about God but to help us to pray to God—pray to the God revealed biblically in Jesus, and not just piously grovel around in some figment of our idolatrous imaginations. Again, that's why Calvin is so useful—he was a pastor/theologian who prayed.

The peace of the Lord,
Eugene

---

*D*ear Gunnar,

I am considerably impressed, and much pleased, that your persistent and prayerful strategies of reconciliation are paying off. Isn't it wonderful how our Lord's grace is able to penetrate these strata of rejection and indifference and hurt that get laid down in the wake of our headlong pursuit of our own interests over the years? Repentance and forgiveness might take a little longer (a lot longer!) to make their mark than violence, but the results are incomparable.

I know you have had good and holy counsel along the way, but still, that your two former wives are now on speaking terms with you, and your two children welcome your visits—after all those years of bitterness and recrimination—well, these are the kinds of miracles that the Christian life specializes in.

And now the only one left is your sister. In going over your letters that describe the difficulties that began as early as adolescence, it seems to me that your goal at this time in your life is simply this: to accept her just the way she is without the expectation that she will ever change. Period. That is the genius of mature love, that it is capable of accepting and embracing without conditions. To think that you have to first establish a certain level of understanding or clear up past differences or develop some strategy so that you can have a "relationship" is going at it from the wrong end of the horse. It means, of course, that you start out admitting limitations, and accepting the fact that you may never get anything out of it, that is, never get anything that might pass for a brother/sister relationship. But if you don't begin by sacrificing all those dreams and illusions, legitimate as they are in motivation, your sister will never have a chance to experience your love. As for your experiencing *her* love, that's her deal, and there is nothing you can do to make it happen.

If you take this approach, the first thing that happens is that the focus leaves your sister. You are now working out of a context of prayer, God's love, your own obedience. Nothing she does or doesn't do is any longer critical to the way you conduct your life and love.

That, as I see it, is the goal. Easy enough for me to say, but how can you pull it off? Not easily. Perhaps not satisfactorily. But if you aren't clear on the goal, you'll spend the rest of your life oscillating between frustration and bitterness.

And what's the alternative? If you are committed because of Jesus to living a life of reconciliation with your estranged family, then it only makes sense to do it in Jesus' way. You have sufficient evidence by now that there is no penetrating that ideological/emotional fortress in which she has taken up residence. There is simply no "reaching" her. But it is possible to love her. Reaching her, anyway, is not a biblical imperative—love is.

Love, at this point in time, probably means to live as courteously as you can manage. Courtesy is not a substitute for love under these conditions, but an elementary form of it. In your situation it is relatively undemanding and so you are not likely to fail at it—you might even become quite good at it and so instead of the guilty or angry frustrations of unreciprocated love, you enjoy the accomplishments of successful courtesy.

Anyway, that's how your "sister-dilemma" looks from this far edge of the continent. Chew on it awhile and see if there is any marrow in the bone.

The peace of the Lord,
Eugene

---

*D*ear Gunnar,

Your reflections on your deacon-assigned visits to the sick and dying are along the lines I had anticipated: a coming to terms with mortality, an embracing of brothers and sisters simply for whom they are, not for what they can produce. We live in a culture that is so determined to eliminate death and weakness from our awareness that it requires a deliberate intervention on our part to maintain some intimate touch with this essential reality of our existence. How distorted our imaginations become if we forget, even for a day or so, that we are going to die.

Amnesia regarding death soon develops into illusions regarding life. Although betrayals of our legacy are frequent, both our Christian Scriptures and traditions insist on facing death as a part of life. We cannot live well if we are not preparing to die well. The old theologians often kept a skull on their writing table to remind them of their mortality. Some monks in the Middle Ages used to sleep in their coffins at night to prevent presuming on another day of life. And you make your weekly visits to your own local Lutheran death row and thereby are unable to wander too far from the neighborhood of both Jesus' death and your own.

Both of us, you realize, are well on our way to approaching the end time of our lives, numbered by the Psalmist as "threescore and ten, or even by reason of strength fourscore" (Psalm 90:10). The closer we get the more the pressure mounts from all sides to avoid or deny the imminence of our deaths. But you have an irrefutable counter-pressure. And, of course, we both have the Eucharist by which we keep faith with both death and life.

The peace of the Lord,
Eugene

---

*D*ear Gunnar,

I have been pondering and praying about what you describe as your slide into dullness, and how much you miss the lightness and sparkle that earlier accompanied your rekindled love for and following of Jesus. You keep asking, "What am I doing wrong?" and I keep ignoring the question, thinking it's just a little speed bump in the road.

I don't, of course, know the deep recesses of your heart and soul, and so cannot in a blanket way say, "You're fine; this is normal; don't worry about it." On the other hand, you have been pretty open with me in this past year since coming back to the faith, and your letters have provided a pretty thorough journal of your prayers and obedience. I think I have a reality base to work with in commenting on your "dullness."

So, aware that we might have to adjust some of these observations if fresh insights arise or new evidence appears, let me say this: Regardless of the feelings you describe, it is highly unlikely that they are a result of bad decisions, wrong moves, or stupid mistakes. In other words, you're not stuck in the mud right now because you didn't read the road map rightly. Which means that you don't have to waste time trying to figure out where you went wrong that ended you up feeling dull and "unspiritual."

If I'm right (and I think the chances are *very* high that I am), it means that we can give our attention to what is going on right now in quite a different way than if we were trying to repair damages or correct mistakes. It means that where you are right now is more in the nature of a biblical wilderness and desert that it is necessary to go through, given the nature of your pilgrimage, given the destination that you set for yourself (or better, that God set for you and you accepted).

So what I am thinking is that we (I'm doing it with you, remember) pay close attention to your environment, this wilderness, and notice the details. Name them. Catalogue them. Nothing, if looked at long enough and closely enough, is without use—not infrequently, beauty unobtrusively seeps into our awareness. And then in the midst of this, while paying attention to what is going on in and around you right now, prayerfully notice what it is showing you about yourself, what is being revealed that you had not noticed before. Things surface in uncongenial circumstances that are able to stay well beneath the surface when everything goes along to your liking. You will make these observations without any thought of doing anything about them or getting rid of them. You will collect your observations by writing them to me. You are training yourself in attentiveness to the conditions in which God's Spirit works.

My assumption behind this counsel (and you don't have to share the assumption) is that what is going on in you right now, given who you are, given what God has done and wants to do in your life, is necessary. It is not a bad intrusion into your otherwise good life, but a necessary passage if you are going to get to Canaan. I know it doesn't feel like that to you. It's sufficient for right now that it feels like that to me.

What do you think? Will you go along with me? I doubt that this will provide quick relief to the joyless tedium in which you seem to be stuck at present. But my sense is that something can come of this that will please us both. There is no true following after Jesus that does not pass through deserts and dark nights.

The peace of the Lord,
Eugene

*D*ear Gunnar,

You seem disappointed that I am not more responsive to your interest in "spiritual direction." Actually, I am more than a little ambivalent about the term, particularly in the ways it is being used so loosely without any sense or knowledge of the church's traditions in these matters.

If by spiritual direction you mean the entering into a friendship with another person in which an awareness and responsiveness to God's Spirit in the everydayness of your life is cultivated, fine. But then why haul in an awkward term like "spiritual direction"? Why not just "friend"?

Spiritual direction strikes me as pretentious in these circumstances, as if there were some expertise that can be acquired more or less on its own and then dispensed on demand.

The other reason for my lack of enthusiasm is my well-founded fear of professionalism in any and all matters of the Christian life. Or maybe the right label for my fear is "functionalism." The moment an aspect of Christian living (human life, for that matter) is defined as a role, it is distorted, debased—and eventually destroyed. We are brothers and sisters with one another, friends and lovers, saints and sinners.

The irony here is that the rise of interest in spiritual direction almost certainly comes from the proliferation of role-defined activism in our culture. We are sick and tired of being slotted into a function and then manipulated with Scripture and prayer to do what someone has decided (often with the help of some psychological testing) that we should be doing to bring glory to some religious enterprise or other. And so when people begin to show up who are interested in us just as we are—our *souls*—

we are ready to be paid attention to in this prayerful, listening, nonmanipulative, nonfunctional way. Spiritual direction.

But then it begins to develop a culture and language and hierarchy all its own. It becomes first a special interest, and then a specialization. That is what seems to be happening in the circles you are frequenting. I seriously doubt that it is a healthy (holy) line to be pursuing.

Instead, why don't you look over the congregation on Sundays and pick someone who appears to be mature and congenial. Ask her or him if you can meet together every month or so—you feel the need to talk about your life in the company of someone who believes that Jesus is present and active in everything you are doing. Reassure the person that he or she doesn't have to say anything "wise." You only want them to be there for you to listen and be prayerful in the listening. After three or four such meetings, write to me what has transpired, and we'll discuss it further.

I've had a number of men and women who have served me this way over the years—none carried the title "spiritual director," although that is what they have been. Some had never heard of such a term. When I moved to Canada a few years ago and had to leave a long-term relationship of this sort, I looked around for someone whom I could be with in this way. I picked a man whom I knew to be a person of integrity and prayer, with seasoned Christian wisdom in his bones. I anticipated that he would disqualify himself. So I pre-composed my rebuttal: "All I want you to do is two things: show up and shut up. Can you do that? Meet with me every six weeks or so, and just be there—an honest, prayerful presence with no responsibility to be anything other than what you have become in your obedient lifetime." And it worked. If that is what you mean by "spiritual director," okay. But I still prefer "friend."

You can see now from my comments that my gut feeling is that the most mature and reliable Christian guidance and understanding comes out of the most immediate and local of settings. The ordinary way. We have to break this cultural habit of sending out for an expert every time we feel we need some assistance. Wisdom is not a matter of expertise.

The peace of the Lord,
Eugene

---

*D*ear Gunnar,

We were at dinner last evening with some friends—five couples of us. All of them actively involved in various social and political programs concerned with poverty and justice in their communities for most of their lives. Conversation more or less circled around fixing the world, and their disappointing experiences in making a difference. Two of them were parents of missionaries in third world settings and pulled in stories of the enormity of the task there. Two were medical doctors, one a forester, all were parents and had raised children who also followed Jesus. They had done this and this and this all their lives, and things were worse than when they had set out full of energy and idealism. The general tone was that the whole thing is pretty hopeless.

I didn't say much. These kind of conversations always seem to me so futile. All these people around the table were Christians, *veteran* Christians, each with at least forty years or so of faithful worship and responsible work behind them. And here's the thing that struck me in the middle of the conversation; not a word in the conversation indicated any awareness of what Christ is doing or has done. It was as if Christmas and Easter and Pentecost had never occurred. None of that got into the conversation. Every person around the table has a highly developed moral/social conscience but not an ounce of theology/spirituality. Our host, Sven, began the meal with a rapidly read "devotional" page from a Lutheran booklet but not so much as a comma from that reading entered into the fabric of the conversation.

Knowing that you would be traveling next week to Geneva to give leadership to your organization of Scientists Against Nuclear Weapons, there was a background awareness of how differently you have been going about this—with neither frenzy nor despair. From the time you first told me of your involvement in this cause, I have appreciated the modest but tenacious ways in which you have taken on what appears to be an impossible task. Don't you think all political and social action has to be done in the larger world that we give witness to in our prayer, "Thy Kingdom come . . ."? Otherwise all we do is end up contributing to the already excessive crankiness and gloom in the world. Know that I'll be praying for you as you lead those meetings, in particular that you will be able to bear witness, whether in silence or otherwise, of a truly *theological* hope for this sin-crossed world that you and your mostly unbelieving friends care so much about.

We live in a Christian ethos that gets its view on salvation from the Bible and its views on the world from the evening news. You at your podium in Geneva and I in my pulpit in Vancouver have our work cut out for us the next few days, don't we?

The peace of the Lord,
Eugene

———————————————————

*D*ear Gunnar,

News around here these days turns on whatever new wildflower just came into blossom. Yesterday it was the moccasin flower, a kind of ladies slipper, orchid-like, that is rare in these parts. But we have a place in the woods that we look for it each year, and usually find it. And then the sightings of returning and migrating birds. We heard the Swainson's thrush for the first time this year three days ago—an ascending organ-like roll that hangs on, reverberating through the pines and hemlocks.

You haven't written for a long time on the ways in which you are finding physical form and structure for your prayers. I always feel that the more physical/material our praying can be, the better: walking, cooking a meal, singing a song, painting a picture, yes, even writing letters!

The peace of the Lord,
Eugene

———————————

*D*ear Gunnar,

So your friends think I'm contradicting myself. The problem is that they are far too rationalistic—they want everything in precisely annotated order. Life is not like that, especially not a holy life, which is life raised to the seventh (or so) power. It's hard to get these things down sequentially, because they do not occur sequentially. I don't think I'm contradicting myself, but I certainly admit to paradox—and considerable ambiguity.

Let me try again. Christian growth (spiritual formation) is, in fact, the easiest thing in the world. This is God's work in Christ through the Spirit in our lives. Grace. We don't have to *do* anything. As a matter of fact, whenever we do get it into our heads to do something, it is usually the wrong thing—we start taking over, running the show, being gods for ourselves and others.

On the other hand, it is the hardest thing in the world, because we are constantly having to get out of the way, to "let it be done unto me according to your word." The faithful, daily return to childlike receiving and obeying, neither of which we initiate, *is* the Christian life.

The troubling thing about so much Christian instruction-for-sale today is that it is little more than self-help psychology with a little holy water sprinkled over it; or the old entrepreneurial American dream fortified with some energizing cheerleader texts.

Much better than trying to summarize steps or stages of Christian development is to immerse ourselves in the grand narratives of our Scriptures—Abraham, Jeremiah, David, Jesus. As we live imaginatively into these lives we start to get the hang of this unique life of the Spirit in which we do less and less so that the Spirit does more and more. The paradox is that while we do less and less, more and more actually gets done through our hands and feet and speech. More energy, less guilt; more of God, less of us. How can you improve on that?

The peace of our Lord,
Eugene

———————————————

*D*ear Gunnar,

So your Pastor has discovered that you are "leadership material" and is determined to get you "involved in ministry." I would have thought you were quite adequately involved simply by entering the place of worship each Sunday and showing up in your laboratory each Monday. I knew this would happen eventually and should have warned you. It was probably your making those deacon-assigned visits to the sick and elderly each month that brought you to his notice. Too bad. And now he wants you to run the new building campaign. Should you do it? By no means.

Pastors are notorious for this kind of thing, but on no account should they be accommodated. I can see why your pastor would ask you to do this—there is a job to be done, and your position and standing in the community set you off as a desirable candidate. Besides, it would provide a showcase to the congregation for your newfound faith and zeal.

Do you know what I think you should do? I think you should take him out to lunch soon and say something like this, "Pastor, you know that I have come back to the Christian way after a long absence. What you might not know is that shortly after my return, and getting my bearings in this new life, I realized that I have also been called into full-time Christian ministry. And I need your help." (This is guaranteed to get his attention!)

"Two things in particular I need from you. First, I need your blessing on my ministry. I have been a research scientist all my working life and, to tell you the truth, never thought for a minute that it was ministry, let alone Christian. But now I do. Actually, it was in the middle of a sermon that you preached that the lights turned on for me. Your text was Jesus and the Gadarene demoniac. You pointed out that after the Gadarene was healed, he quite naturally wanted to join up with Jesus and his disciples in their ministry, but that Jesus wouldn't let him, but said, "Go home to your family and tell them how much the Lord has done for you, and how he has had mercy on you" (Mark 5:19).

"In the immediate context of my life, 'family' translated into my daily work. And so I did it. Nothing I have done as a Christian has seemed more clearly an act of obedience. But even though clear, it is not easy, for none of my associates at work nor my new Christian friends understand it as ministry. I'm beginning to feel very isolated, even beleaguered. That's why I need your blessing—your blessing and your prayers, validating and strengthening me in my full-time Christian ministry.

"The second thing I need is your protection. This is demanding work and requires much concentration and energy. The longer I am in this church the more I feel that people here are distracting and diverting me from my ministry. If I lived out my Christian faith the way they think I should, I would end up simply putting in 'secular' hours at the laboratory and saving up my 'Christian' energies for evening meetings and weekend church projects. If I am to keep at this Christian ministry of mine full-time, I need your help in protecting me from well-meaning interference from others. That's why I can't take this position you are asking me to fill and why I need your support and understanding in saying no."

I'm sure that you are going to say this more tactfully than I am writing it. I wish I could figure out a way to get the ear of all the laypeople, *God's* people of North

America, and tell them: Go to your pastors and tell them that you want them to be your preachers and intercessors, period. Then lock them in their studies or oratories. Tell them that you want them to do their work, not yours. Get them out of your life. Tell them to quit interfering in your ministry and get on with their own. Their work is no more important than yours, nor is yours than theirs—they are equally important. Tell them that you respect the integrity of their work and you want them to respect the integrity of yours. Tell them that you need help to do your work, but the help you need is not to be told what to do or how to do it. Tell them you are tired of being condescended to, of being viewed as an adjunct to their ministry. Tell them that you have been called to a ministry every bit as important and certainly as demanding as theirs. And you need help, all the help you can get. But the help you need is the word of God preached with imagination and conviction. Tell them you need to be prayed for with passion and faithfulness and listened to without distraction or hurry.

My fantasy is to collect a million signatures and place it as a broadside in all the leading newspapers of North America. Will you sign it?

I'm on a bit of a soapbox, I know, but if Christian ministry is reduced to the work of pastors and the people who help them out evenings and weekends, there is not much integrity in praying "Thy Kingdom Come," is there?

The peace of the Lord,
Eugene

*D*ear Gunnar,

Finding time to pray is a primary challenge, maybe *the* primary challenge, for the contemporary Christian. The Devil and all his angels are working full-time in a conspiracy to fill up the hours of each day with urgent duties, responsible enterprises, and, if we should happen to find ourselves unemployed in some odd hour or other, frivolous distractions. Even our friends and pastors seem, more often than not, to be partners in the conspiracy.

That fact that this is happening at a time and in a culture in which we are surfeited with labor-saving devices, and, in North America at least, have a standard of living that technically permits considerable leisure, indicates that the problem has little to do with "finding time" to pray and more with learning how to pray in adverse conditions—conditions in which we are taught that time is a commodity ("time is money") rather than an aspect of God's eternity.

That also is why I think you are going at it from the wrong end. You don't "find time" to pray by arranging and then re-arranging your schedule. The very first thing to do in finding time to pray is to throw away your Daytimer.

I mean it. Throw it away. Your Daytimer may be very useful for organizing the world's work and your social calendar, getting you to your job on time, and showing up for appointments you've agreed upon. But it has a negative effect on your praying life because it reinforces the sense that time is a quantitative thing that you control when in fact it is a vast dimension of creation that you find yourself in.

I would encourage you to re-conceive your day as a ritual—a rhythmic sequence of movements in sacred space and time—which you enter, rather than as a schedule into which you fit yourself. Schedules are wooden, inflexible, static, impersonal. Rituals are elastic, spacious, dynamic, and participatory.

You either keep to a schedule or don't. But a ritual is capable of infinite variations and adaptations—the proportions and movement are the thing, the relationships, the encounters, the rhythms. Fitting prayer into a schedule is like trying to fit God into a schedule. The schedule is the secularization of the ritual and the Daytimer is its Bible.

I know that there are many practical details that have to be met and decided upon; I'm not oblivious to any of them (I do always show up on time for our occasionally arranged visits in Denver, don't I?). But I am convinced that regarding prayer, the most significant thing we can do begins in the imagination: seeing the day (week, month, year) as a ritual in which we are entering, responding, and participating in the ways of God. *Not* carving out time for God—how condescending that sounds!

I'm not saying that rituals are easier than schedules. Hardly! They are much more difficult and require much attention and discipline—just as dancing a ballet requires far more of you than marching in the infantry. What I am saying is that something like a ritual is the only way in which we will ever have adequate and leisurely time and space for prayer. Yes, throw away your Daytimer; it's the only way you'll ever get a chance at coming upon what Paul meant when he said, "Pray without ceasing."

The peace of the Lord,
Eugene

_____

Dear Gunnar,

I'm sorry that your friend you brought to church last week was so put off by the grim faces she found there. But I wouldn't be too upset by it. We're not in charge of publicity for the Almighty. Besides, neither Minnesota weather nor Norwegian upbringing (and especially not in combination!) exactly encourages spiritual boosterism. Tell her that if she sticks around Christians awhile, even Lutheran Christians, she'll find plenty of people to both laugh at and with. We have a huge roster of "saints" whose stories and antics can enliven the grimmest of congregations.

Tell her the story of St. Teresa of Ávila, who lived in a very humorless century. She disdained frivolity, but her good humor was irrepressible. (This story is probably apocryphal, but is completely in character.) The Spanish saint was in the outhouse one day, reading her prayers and eating a muffin. The Devil appeared and scolded her: "How unspiritual! How abominably sacrilegious!" Teresa shot back, "The prayer is for God, the muffin is for me, and the rest is for you."

The peace of the Lord,
Eugene

---

*D*ear Gunnar,

Sorry, but that's not a good idea, not a good idea at all. Choosing a spiritual director or advisor who is immersed in Jungian spirituality is foolishness at the least and catastrophic at the worst.

I am quite aware that Carl Jung is the spiritual director of choice for a large company of our contemporaries. But however spiritual he is, he is quite definitely not Christian. Anyone can learn much about the human psyche from him, but all his marvelous insights are without context, without commitment, without responsibility.

Jung vehemently rejected the Christian way and was indifferent to morals. He would have no truck with the God revealed in Jesus Christ (although he was full of "divinity" talk) and acted as if he were in charge of his own sovereign desires—went to bed with anyone he fancied, lied whenever it suited him, and pretty much carried on as his own wonderful god. He gutted the vocabulary of spirituality of the strong, sharp-edged Christian words such as sin, repentance, obedience, judgment, salvation, sacrifice, glory—not to mention Father, Son, and Holy Spirit!—and replaced them with his boozy archetypes, that account for everything without the inconvenience of God and Sinai and Calvary.

I'm not, of course, saying that his lack of theology and morality discredits his insights. The insights are valuable and useful. But without a context in theology and morality—in biblical revelation—they leave us without context in God and the moral life. And God is, after all, the one with whom we have to do. And the moral life, after all, provides the warp and woof for weaving a holy life.

Learn what you can from Jung and his followers. But keep your distance from their personal influence on you.

You're a lot safer drinking coffee with one of your dull but devout farmer friends than getting high on the verbal drugs of the glamorous Jung.

The peace of the Lord,
Eugene

———————————————

*D*ear Gunnar,

So, he "flunked churchgoing" did he? A colorful way of putting it. But also in the circumstances blunt and honest. I know it disappoints you that your son hasn't found the same grounding in reality and "habit of being" in the church that you have. But be patient. Remember, when you were his age you would never have admitted to "flunking churchgoing"—you were claiming to have *graduated* from it.

My sense is that plain churchgoing is one of the most difficult things for Christians to do these days—especially for young, inexperienced new converts like your son. The early church was totally counterculture, and so there was almost always a sense of exhilaration, of *definition* that created an alert Christian mindset for both danger and grace. Many third-world churches still have that. But the contemporary church (at least in North America) is doing its level best to accommodate itself to the culture. Deep within, beneath the secularizing veneer, it's still the church, but the "bite" has gone. "Church" seems neither daring nor dangerous. I can understand your son's sense of letdown.

There are stages in the soul's pilgrimage in which we are ultrasensitive to the blasphemy of trivia and have virtually no tolerance for nonsense. And since there is always plenty of trivia and nonsense when sinners get together, when we are unprepared for this, it's better simply to absent ourselves until we acquire strength adequate for coping.

The fact is that it takes a mature Christian these days to make it in church. You have a forty-year head start on your son. Those years of search and pain, losing your life and then finding it, prepared you to enter the church as one sinner among others, grateful for every scrap of grace and salvation that came your way in Word and Sacrament. Anders still thinks it ought to be some kind of utopian society of nice people where holiness is some kind of "high."

Give him a few years. At some point he will realize that he can't be his own preacher and priest, and that God hides his glory in the oddest places—in a carpenter's shop, a fishing boat, a washbasin, a supper table, yes, even in a church. Meanwhile, I wouldn't badger him about it.

The peace of the Lord,
Eugene

_____

*D*ear Gunnar,

Your delight in coming across that monastery isolated out there on those austere plains, "miles from nowhere," and finding a community of praying brothers there is contagious. I am more and more convinced that holiness does infiltrate *place*. In such places, I always have a sense of homecoming—*heaven*-coming. We necessarily live much of our lives in exile, so to be able to spot the people and places that re-establish our true identity is *so* important. I hope you'll be able to get out there at least a couple of times a year.

The peace of the Lord,
Eugene

———————————————

*D*ear Gunnar,

   I loved your description of your day on the river, canoeing with your daughter. I've never been on your northern Minnesota rivers—I'd love to do it with you sometime. Don't you think the canoe is the most contemplative device for travel ever constructed? On the same day (I think it was the same day), Jan and I spent five hours hiking on a mountain trail that we like a lot. It was raining lightly the whole time, but there was a kind of reflected luminosity that brought out the brilliant coloring in the just-emerging wildflowers. I don't think we have ever seen the alpine wildflowers quite so profuse. And then, after more or less staggering from one explosion of beauty to another, Jan spotted a small, brightly colored bird perched on a dead snag. We looked and looked—had never seen anything like it. All red and orange. And then it flew and we recognized it as a hummingbird. We identified it later as a *rufous*—a first sighting for us.

   Aren't we lucky to have so many visible confirmations of the invisible graces within us?

The peace of the Lord,
Eugene

────────────────────

*D*ear Gunnar,

I hope you are able (and wanting) to keep this letter-writing going. There are complex and intricate things taking place in your body and spirit, your work and your church these days. And while you have received some extraordinary graces recently, there are going to be some pretty long and dry stretches ahead. There always are. An established pattern of writing (it could be conversation if we lived in the same town) lets me prayerfully attend to your life. At the same time, it relieves you of the burden of having to anxiously watch and interpret and evaluate every feeling and opinion that comes up. You can just enjoy (or not!) more or less as you feel like it, as the Spirit develops the strengths and virtues necessary for living to His glory in this seventh decade of your life.

The peace of the Lord,
Eugene

_____

*D*ear Gunnar,

I was visiting a friend over the July Fourth weekend and went to church with him. It was a skillfully and elaborately orchestrated blend of nostalgia, Americana, and holy water. It came to a rousing climax with the organ playing a let-out-all-the-stops rendition of "The Stars and Stripes Forever" while a large American flag slowly ascended from underground, filling the entire chancel. The service ended with everyone on their feet, applauding. I was, as you can imagine, not amused and couldn't seem to get my hands out of my pockets.

Somehow I don't think this is what Jesus meant when he said, "Render to Caesar the things that are Caesar's and to God the things that are God's."

Your letters, by the way (have I commented on this before?), are sounding more and more to me like acts of prayer—the honest, unpretentious acts of attention that you give to your work and your worship, your children and your colleagues—and seem to me less and less concerned with you, and more and more alert to the way the Holy Spirit is revealing grace and shaping holiness.

The peace of the Lord,
Eugene

*D*ear Gunnar,

Why on earth would anyone think to ask you to be advisor to the church young people? And why would you ever accept? I can't think of anyone *less* qualified. You have spent the last forty or so years in more or less adolescent rebellion against God. Your own children are only slowly recovering from the misinformation and distortions with which you so carelessly fed their souls in the years of their growing up.

On the other hand, your very *dis*qualification might constitute your qualification. (This happens quite a lot in Christian spirituality!) At least you are under no illusions about the purity of the adolescent spirit and are probably well-inoculated against picking up and passing around silly slogans like "our youth are the church of the future." On the contrary—and you know this as well as I do from long years of dealing with this—the adolescent experience is adept at taking almost any item in Christian belief and behavior and flipping it on its head, so that it ends up functioning quite contrary to anything given to us in the Gospel. And quite often to the applause of adults who should know better, but who are having their socks charmed off of them by the fresh enthusiasm and melodramatic demands of these as-yet-unformed Christians. Since youth is obviously a critical time in which life decisions are made that can well shape the rest of our lives, certain leaders in the church began lobbying us to pay special attention to our youth so that we can "keep" them in the fold and insure their Christian commitment.

Here is another of those sea-changes that has taken place in the North American church during your long absence from it—this specialized concentration on youth ministry. The entire youth culture of North America was targeted as a primary missionary field, and many of those who have worked the field can be numbered among the most single-minded and sacrificial servants of Jesus in our time. Many, many good things have resulted from the ministries of the men and women who have given themselves to this work—in fact, some of the most daring and sacrificial Christian work in our time has taken place in this area. But there is a negative aspect to it as well. (This is not uncommon in spirituality—we do something really well, and that excellence is then used as a cover for something quite undesirable, and nobody notices for quite a long time.)

The hitch is this: In the very act of concentrating/specializing on youth, the two very worst features of adolescence are more or less sanctioned: the self-absorption and the cultishness. Adolescence is a plunge into selfism, and adolescence develops (if permitted) a sense of cultic purity and superiority to the prevailing adult culture. What we hope for in our young people is to get them through the selfishness and cultishness, not collaborate with them in it.

So what's happened without anyone really intending it is this widespread adaptation of the Christian Gospel to appeal to the worst features of youth: Jesus is presented as the key to having fun and fulfilling your*self*; as a consequence this exciting youth "culture" becomes the norm for the rest of the church. Result: an adolescent church of Peter Pan Christians who don't ever want to grow up.

It's a pretty far cry, I can tell you, from the conversations Jesus had with his disciples as he prepared to sacrifice himself for them and initiate them into a similar life of sacrifice and salvation.

Your congregation doesn't know how lucky they are to be too poor to afford a youth worker and end up stuck with you—you who are bored to death with youth as such but seem to have endless patience with those people, of whatever ages, who show signs of wanting to discover (or recover) how God in Christ is present and working in their lives.

But I wandered off the track a bit didn't I? You got me off on this by asking for some direction in working with the youth in your congregation. One idea occurred to me as I was going on about the negative effect of "youth ministry" in our churches. But you'll have to wait a couple of days; right now I have to make my hospital visits. Meanwhile, know that you have my respect and prayers for venturing into "fool-for-Christ" territory.

The peace of the Lord,
Eugene

———————————————

*D*ear Gunnar,

What I have in mind for you in your new job as adult youth advisor to those seven or eight Norwegian teenagers is simply this: Invite them over to your home to cook a meal with you. Make it a regular thing, say, once every couple of weeks. And that's it.

But there is more to it than meets the eye. First, it's something you like to do and are good at. You have that huge country farm kitchen, furnished with every conceivable cooking device—in a culture of fast-food and efficiency, your kitchen opens up a world of care for food and its painstaking preparation will strike them, to use one of their words, as awesome. Second, you will be taking them seriously as persons, without any condescending adaptation to their status as adolescents. You are inviting them into your adult world and making them participants in it—work that is not make-work; work, not entertainment (although not without its pleasures). Third, you will be working out of a context of hospitality, probably the very best setting in which to develop personal relationships and develop conversations that include Jesus. Do you realize how much of Jesus' ministry took place around cooking and eating? Without making a point of it, these young people will realize that you are taking them seriously, not as adolescents, but simply as themselves as they share in the preparation of the meal and join in the eating of it. My wife often says (she is quoting somebody but can never remember who it is) that true hospitality is when an onlooker can't distinguish between the host and the guest. Having a book or two around that one of you could read aloud while waiting for a pot to boil or potato to bake might fuel later conversation.

You have scores of delightful and sometimes imaginatively complex recipes—they're not likely to get bored. And you will have provided a setting in which they will experience themselves in ways which are rare for them: treated with dignity, not exploited to some program or other, and treated as "souls" to be nurtured, not psyches to be fixed.

I can easily imagine something like this developing quite naturally outwards. Every so often you could prepare a huge pot of soup and take it to downtown Moorhead or Fargo and help out with one of the street missions to the hungry and homeless. When a person or family shows up in worship on Sunday, any one of the youth is free to invite them over for supper—you have a ready-made occasion for hospitality at hand and available, a far sight better than those "visitor" ribbons that get slapped onto strangers in so many of our churches.

I'm sure, by now, you can discern the conviction that is behind my suggestion: that "ministry" is organic, growing out of who and where we are in the circumstances in which we know and serve Jesus; *not* something we impose on a person or setting as "mission" or "evangelism" or "youth ministry."

When you get around to making bouillabaisse, try and get me invited, even though I qualify as neither hungry nor a stranger.

The peace of the Lord,
Eugene

---

*D*ear Gunnar,

Do you think "disciplines" is quite the right word for what you are after? Why not simply "prayer"? I hesitate to throw cold water on your enthusiasm, but I would be less than honest if I didn't let you in on my reservations. Anything we do to counter the flabbiness, the casualness, the frivolity that characterizes so much of our culture is to the good, but trying to develop expertise in any aspect of the Christian life has a way of seducing us into supposing that "here, at least, is *one* thing that gives me an edge over my neighbors, and a little extra approval from God."

What we have to guard against is technology—a way of doing something, even for God, that separates us from relationship with God and our need of mercy. As with so much else in life, we must learn how to accept and practice the good in the right way, otherwise it turns bad. Food is good, but too much of it makes us fat. Sex is good, but wrongly practiced is bad. Labor is good, but forced labor is slavery.

While the world is out there developing competency on a thousand fronts, we Christians stubbornly stay at home cultivating a sense of incompetence in our own backyards (the old word for it is humility).

The peace of the Lord,
Eugene

———————————

*D*ear Gunnar,

Do I get the sense that this long, slow slog you have been plodding through this last several months is lightening up a bit? At least you now have a sense of movement—*going* somewhere instead of falling into no place.

One of the things that I have reflected upon recently is how *biblical* the feeling of godforsakeness is . . . "Why have you forsaken me?"! How frequently this kind of language occurs in Psalms before Jesus picks it up and prays it definitively. And how often—always?—it leads us eventually into a new spaciousness and freedom, into green pastures. When this is all over you are going to be mighty glad to be done with that old religious self that kept interfering and taking charge and getting in the way.

And do I get a sense that you are even starting to *enjoy* the process? Delighting in the glimpses of largeness and openness that lie ahead? I got a letter from a friend recently who has lived through several months of what you are (hopefully) at the outer edge of. Her words: "I've learned new definitions of hope in these past few months. Hope is not so much a noun or a verb. Rather, it is deeper than that. It is the syntax which binds life together into meaning. . . . In a more 'human' image, hope is that picture of being held like a child, held and led by the hand. My twenty years of nursing had knocked all such 'hope' out of me. I feel like I've had a hope transplant, and it is growing again—a little 'plant' of hope!"

I like that; it moves hope beyond mere optimism or wishful thinking into something deeper and more eternal—into God.

The peace of the Lord,
Eugene

---

*D*ear Gunnar,

I think I know what you mean when you say that you could do without all this "religious stuff." I take it by "stuff" you mean the late-night church council meetings, the trivializing budget arguments, the denominational pronouncements that read like they were conceived on another planet, the church politics; I guess I agree. I have never had much stomach for "religion" as such myself. But I don't think either you nor I can do without it. As Flannery O'Connor writes someplace, "The fleas come with the dog."

It helps me to make a rough distinction between "religion" and "spirituality." By religion I mean the efforts that we make to keep things together in a somewhat orderly fashion, to maintain some sense of responsibility before God. By spirituality I mean the work of the Holy Spirit in making Jesus alive in us, inciting us to acts of love and compassion, blessing us with his gifts, bringing us to our knees in repentance and up on our feet in wonder. Religion is mostly a matter of what we do; spirituality is mostly a matter of what God does. My own practice has been to keep my involvement in religion to a responsible minimum—my participation in spirituality (in the Spirit!) extravagantly maximal.

It is understandable that people who have had a heavy dose of manipulative, controlling, oppressive, or boring religion should look for a spirituality that is "pure." But they're never going to find it. There have been a lot of ventures in our long Christian history of people who have tried to create what they think of as an uncontaminated spirituality. They always end up with something worse than they rejected. They always end up as one more variation on the age-old do-your-own-thing-spirituality—mostly ego, very little God. Ego Spirituality. We're afflicted with an epidemic of it these days.

A number of years ago, when I was able, I used to attend vespers with a community of Benedictine nuns. I loved the quiet simplicity of the worship, the nuns anonymous in their habits, the liturgy so natural and unforced. It always seems much more spiritual than the religious fuss and murkiness of my Presbyterian congregation. I got to know one of the nuns quite well. One day in conversation she must have detected the romanticizing envy in me and said, "You think we're in ecstasy all the time in here don't you, Eugene? You probably think we levitate while we are washing up the dishes! Well, let me tell you something. We are a community of saints and martyrs—and the martyrs are the ones who have to live with the saints!" That cured me—for awhile, at least.

Actually, I've been most pleased with the way you have gone about it the last couple of years: a willing but modest involvement in the religious affairs of the congregation, but maintaining a keen and insatiable appetite for God's Word and Spirit across a wide spectrum of circumstance and experience and with a surprising assortment of people.

The peace of the Lord,
Eugene

Dear Gunnar,

I don't think you should worry overmuch about your daughter's dabbling in New Age concepts. Not much of it stands the test of reality for very long, and she strikes me as a pretty no-nonsense person. Take their basic doctrine, for instance, of "All roads lead to God"—do any of them really believe that the satanic ritual abuser, the fundamentalist Islamic suicide bomber, and the communist terrorist, all intensely religious, are all alike on the road that leads to God?

Our position is "Any place is the right place to start for God." Nothing in your belief, behavior, or circumstance disqualifies you from starting toward God. I've always liked the way St. John juxtaposes the orthodox and pious Nicodemus and the heretical and rather disreputable Samaritan woman (John 3 and 4), and demonstrates that both positions are equally valid for beginning a life with Jesus.

Judith is poised at a starting place, not stuck in a dead-end. Your prayers, not your arguments, will be your most useful action right now. And I'll join you in the prayers.

The peace of the Lord
Eugene

---

*D*ear Gunnar,

Your Bible Study group is one of the wonders of the world. How you ever managed to get such an ill-sorted melange of misfits together and weave a community of prayer and conversation among them, I'll never know: two farmers, a recent widow, a Downs Syndrome young man, that dour history professor, the mother who would rather be a poet than raise her kids, and the young athlete who has become the darling of Minnesota as she emerges suddenly as the top woman golfer in the midwest (and isn't handling the media attention very well). The descriptions you send to me (when you remember to do it!) of the insights and probes, the relationships and prayer that take place week by week as you plod through Mark's gospel are always a delight to read. "Soul-fatting" was the old Puritan expression for it.

I say it is "one of the wonders of the world," which it most certainly is. But it is not at all uncommon. This kind of thing is taking place all over the world, all the time. This biblical text of ours is the most accessible, most life-giving, most community-making book ever written. There is nothing quite like it—and your experience is one more validation (as if I needed another!) of what happens when a few Christians deliberately put themselves under its influence, prayerfully and obediently. It quite transcends matters of intelligence and sophistication (as your group attests). One of the most perceptive Bible students I have ever been with was a truck driver who was nearly illiterate—but he had good ears. Oh, how he listened!

So I can imagine how dismaying and disruptive it is to have your newly assigned seminary summer intern, Herman, decide to join your group and "teach" you how to study the Bible, intoxicated as he is with his "histori-cal/critical" tools by which he takes the Bible apart, piece by piece, and thinks he's doing you a favor by sorting all its parts into little piles of verbs and potsherds. Reading your description of Herman's performance, I remembered Gandalf's comment in *The Lord of the Rings*: "... he that breaks a thing to find out what it is has left the path of wisdom." This kind of thing has nearly ruined Bible study for many Christians in our time. You as a layman and I as a pastor need to stand fast against it, lest we lose access to the one sure thing, God's Word in our language, that we have to contribute to our un-godded world. The difficulty is not in *what* he is telling, but in his manner and timing. All these tools for Bible study that seminarians are taught are useful—and if you are going to spend your life behind a lectern or a pulpit, most valuable. But they are delicate surgical instruments that require much care and wisdom in their exercise. It appears to me that he is using them as sledgehammers and crowbars.

There may be nothing you can do about it—put up with him and love him for the next three months. Maybe your group can accommodate even the likes of him! But by no means are you to be intimidated by him. This modern tendency to defer to the authority of experts, particularly in matters of soul, has to be resisted on all fronts. The Bible is first of all the people's book, not the professor's or the pastor's.

The peace of the Lord,
Eugene

*D*ear Gunnar,

While taking my early morning walk a couple of days ago, I thought of something out of our high school years that may help understand Herman and why his thoughtless and well-intentioned "help" is so unhelpful.

Remember Oscar Odegaard, Bucky Jones, and that crowd? And the year they formed a gun club and began meeting every week, fondling their guns, engaging in target practice, and entering marksmanship competitions? And how puzzled you and I were over the whole business?

Virtually every adolescent young man in that culture, of course, had a gun. It was a "gun culture"—our emerging "wild west" identity wasn't complete without a gun. But for you and me and most of our friends the gun was part of something larger—hunting and hiking, mountains and streams, pheasants and ducks, deer and antelope. The gun was our ticket to that intricate and unpredictable world of weather and wildness and youthful camaraderie. It hardly mattered that we shot anything—and more often than not we didn't. The gun symbolized and made possible our participation in a certain kind of *life*.

The gun club struck us as so *reductionist*. That seasonally comprehensive, sensually rich, unpredictable life of the woods and rivers was eliminated in the interests of accuracy and control. Actually, they were probably better shots than we were, at least if there was no sleet stinging their eyes. But it struck us as mighty boring. And then the airs of superiority that they assumed—buying special jackets, making sure their trophies were well displayed, and acting just the least bit condescending to the rest of us.

Does it strike you that that may be what Herman is doing with the Bible? Removing it from the complex context of saints and sinners, of doubt and faith, of suffering and bewilderment so that he can render it *accurately*? But the Bible came into existence in the rough and tumble of sin and salvation among ordinary people. It has never seemed to me especially honoring to it to insist on interpreting it in sanitary laboratory conditions. All the learning that Herman brings to the Bible is useful, but if he doesn't enter the "conditions" as he reads and teaches it, he'll never get it right. Just don't let him turn your wonderful Bible study into a "gun club."

The peace of the Lord,
Eugene

———————————

*D*ear Gunnar,

I think it's best to stay simple and centered in regards to prayer. Development in prayer doesn't come through acquired techniques but through a growing intimacy with the Father, revealed in Jesus, by the Spirit. Put that way, you can see immediately how *relational* prayer is (having to do with *persons*), and how much it has to do with God, who is far more active in your prayers than you are.

Most Christians for most centuries have taken the Psalms as their basic prayer text and prayed them, finding in such praying an immersion in the entire range of the human condition and the incredibly varied ways in which God meets us. You seem to have taken to this common way like a duck to water.

My suggestion now is to add to that the daily meditation upon and praying of the Lord's Prayer. The Psalms give range and variety; the Lord's Prayer gives brevity and focus. I would avoid reading what other people write about it at this point in your life: explore and discover for yourself. The Prayer is endlessly revealing of God's heart and the ways in which we can respond and participate in his being and action. Take the six (or seven) petitions and let them shape your day and week. Don't be afraid of rote repetitions—the prayer, frequently repeated, can, if you let it, work itself into your muscles and memory (actually, the Spirit does the working).

Most of our honored teachers of the past, when they set about instructing their congregations in the Christian life, simply taught them the Lord's Prayer. Prayer is not what you do on your knees; it is what you *live*. Your knees can function as a fulcrum to your prayers, but our intent always is that our life is our prayer.

I just don't want you to waste any of your precious time chasing after the fads and fashions of contemporary religion. The old ways are better.

The peace of our Lord,
Eugene

———————————————

*D*ear Gunnar,

So, you "got an offer you can't refuse," did you? My knee-jerk reaction to such offers is to refuse them outright. You can be sure that the company that made the offer didn't pray about it and, in fact, is looking at you only in terms of your reputation and economic value to them. I hate to think of you making a major decision about your life simply by calculating its dollar value.

Implicit in your letter is a question that I think is put wrongly. Reading between the lines, I hear you asking whether we ought to do what brings wholeness/happiness to our lives, or whether we should ignore that, look at the needs around us, decide on what takes precedence, grit our teeth, and go to it. It's not precisely either/or.

Two things need to be brought out on the table. One, God does will our wholeness, our peace, our completion in his love/salvation. Pain is not a spiritual attribute. Discomfort is not a sign that we are doing God's will. A hard life is not evidence that we are carrying the cross of Jesus. These are all pagan ideas that have fogged our minds and need to be dismissed.

On the other hand, our happiness, as such, is not a good criterion either. Often we don't know what is best for us. We are immature; we are sinners; we are self-centered. And so very often, what we would choose out of self-interest is, in fact, counter to our best interest—which is Christ in us. And so sacrifice is also at the center of our lives—setting ourselves believingly before God so that we can be Christ-formed, not self-made.

So how are you to make your decision? Much as you are going at it right now, I guess. Anticipating blessing and fullness but willing to sacrifice immediate gratification to what God wills to do through you. Clarification often comes through humble means, like writing and receiving letters, through conversations with friends, deliberately letting the act of Lord's Day worship establish the boundaries and size of your life. Somewhere in the midst of this prayerfulness you will make your decision (without any guarantee that it is absolutely right). And then God gives grace to live out what is decided.

Just make sure you give equal weight to your new friends, your remarkable (but so humble!) church, the beauties of woods and weather and set it all in scales against that flattering offer. I've seen too many of my friends' lives impoverished by a big salary.

The peace of the Lord,
Eugene

———————————————

*D*ear Gunnar,

After two weeks of brutal cold, it began snowing early this morning. These low-lying, sun-eclipsing clouds finally decided to release their treasures. Snowfall is so filled with silence, a soft, textured, palpable silence, don't you think? It's just as cold as before, but it's not the same—there is more to cold than a centigrade reading. The snow has transformed the flat, dull, cold into something storied, like a quilt. An invitation to turn the raw facts of winter into the stories of Advent and Christmas.

But we have some friends coming to dinner in a couple of hours, so instead of rhapsodizing over the freshly sculptured world, I better get out and start interfering with the inconvenience of so much beauty and get a path shoveled.

The peace of the Lord,
Eugene

---

*D*ear Gunnar,

Do you have any idea how much delight it gives me when you write about your church? After all these years of absence you return to Christ and immediately head for the closest congregation of Christians—that obscure, little band of Lutherans on the edge of town—and simply make yourself at home among them. And not only settling in but *relishing* their company.

I wonder if you have any idea how rare that is. You had a bit of a rocky start, but now you are *there*.

The Christian congregation is the whipping boy of our culture these days. Not so much of the secular culture—they mostly ignore churches. But of Christians themselves. You would have no way of knowing this, of course, but pastors are the worst. Some of the most dismaying conversations I have are in gatherings of pastors, most of whom either bitch or brag about their churches, depending on whether they are flourishing or languishing as religious businesses. And then the people pick up the evaluations and attitudes and continue to pass them around.

Maybe your forty years on the outside cured you of that kind of approach. By this time you're fed up with a world of glamour and prestige and achievement, having realized it is mostly illusion. And so when you entered a congregation, having discovered that faith has to do first of all with invisibles, you were ready to see all that rich and burgeoning *invisibility* in that unpretentious gaggle of Norwegians that come together on Sunday mornings, a little stiff, still, in their rectitude and decidedly awkward in their worship. Anyway, you cheer my heart as you give witness to the work and presence of the Holy Spirit among the very people in Moorhead where journalists (and on-the-make pastors?) would never think to look for it.

When I read your Sunday morning reports I often remember the couplet of Richard Wilbur's. Do you know it?

> *My eye shall never know the dry disease,*
> *Of thinking things no more than what it sees.*

Several years ago I was away from my congregation on a Sabbatical year and instead of leading in worship was led in worship Sunday after Sunday. I had always thought that the most important thing I did each week was call people to worship; but I sometimes wondered if I overvalued it simply because it was *my* work. But I discovered that it was just as important to be led in worship as to lead it.

Very often when I left the place of worship the first impression I had of the "outside world" was how small it was—how puny its politics, paltry its appetites, squint-eyed its interests. I had just spent an hour or so with friends reorienting myself in the realities of the world—the huge sweep of salvation and the minute particularities of holiness—and would blink my eyes in disbelief that so many are willing to live in such reduced and cramped conditions. But after a few hours or days, I found myself getting used to and going along with its assumptions since most of the politicians and journalists, artists and entertainers, stockbrokers and shoppers seem to assume that that was the real world. And then Sunday would come around again, and some pastor would call me back to reality, "Let us worship God." And I would get it straight again, see it whole.

Every call to worship is a call into the Real World. You'd think by this time in my life I wouldn't need to be called any more. But I do. I encounter such constant and widespread lying about reality each day and meet with such skilled and systematic distortion of the truth that I'm always in danger of losing my grip on reality. The reality, of course, is that God is sovereign and Christ is savior. The reality is that prayer is my mother tongue and the Eucharist my basic food. The reality is that baptism, not Myers-Briggs, defines who I am. The reality is, as Leon Bloy so poignantly put it, that "the only sadness is not to be a saint."

But I don't find many around me who see it this way. I seem to be part of a dwindling minority (although counting the people in cemeteries, I'm pretty sure I'm part of a larger roll call). Most of the people I hear talk about this have no patience for Invisibilities and less skill in detecting them. They can't be bothered with noticing and appreciating what is already there, so determined they are to re-shape "church" into something more to their liking.

So you can see how much you have meant to me since your conversion (or re-conversion), initiating these conversations and reclaiming the old camaraderie of our youth, re-establishing the amazing Jesus-gift of "friend," and joining me as an ally in the Real World.

The peace of the Lord,
Eugene

Other Books in the Growing Deeper Series You Will Enjoy